CHILDREN OF THE HOLOCAUST

by Stephanie Fitzgerald

Content Adviser:
Harold Marcuse, PhD,
Associate Professor, Department of History,
University of California, Santa Barbara

Reading Adviser:
Alexa Sandmann, EdD,
Professor of Literacy, College and Graduate School
of Education, Health, and Human Services, Kent State University

COMPASS POINT BOOKS
a capstone imprint

Compass Point Books
151 Good Counsel Drive
P.O. Box 669
Mankato, MN 56002-0669

Editor: Brenda Haugen
Designer: Ashlee Suker
Media Researcher: Svetlana Zhurkin
Library Consultant: Kathleen Baxter
Production Specialist: Sarah Bennett
Cartographer: XNR Productions, Inc.

On the cover:
Jewish children, survivors of Auschwitz, with a nurse behind a barbed wire fence in February 1945

Image Credits
akg-images/Benno Gantner, 50; DVIC/NARA, 49, 59 (bottom); Getty Images: Anne Frank
House, 37, Galerie Bilderwelt, cover, Hulton Archive, 14, 42, 59 (top), Hulton Archive/Kurt
Hutton, 21, Picture Post/Gerti Deutsch, 19, 22, Popperfoto, 45, Popperfoto/Paul Popper, 12, Time
Life Pictures/Hugo Jaeger, 27; Newscom, 54; United States Holocaust Memorial Museum: 28,
courtesy of Ada Nissim, 31, courtesy of Bep Meyer Zion, 36, courtesy of David Tennenbaum, 32,
courtesy of Dorrith Oppenheim Sim, 10, courtesy of Genevieve Tyrangiel-Benezra, 34, courtesy of
Lydia Chagoll, 16, 58, courtesy of Mayer and Rachel Abramowitz Harold Fishbein, 56, courtesy of
Moshe Zilbar, 24, courtesy of Richard Freimark, 5, courtesy of Ruth Sherman, National Archives
and Records Administration, Ministere des Anciens Combattants et Victimes de Guerre, 52,
courtesy of Vivette Herman Samuel, 39, Henry Schwarzbaum, 46, National Archives and Records
Administration, 48, National Archives and Records Administration, Centre de Documentation Juive
Contemporaine, 44, National Archives and Records Administration, Yad Vashem Photo Archives, 8,
Yad Vashem, Panstwowe Muzeum w Oswiecim-Brzezinka, 41.

 This book was manufactured with paper containing
at least 10 percent post-consumer waste.

Library of Congress Cataloging-in-Publication Data
Fitzgerald, Stephanie.
    Children of the Holocaust / by Stephanie Fitzgerald.
        p. cm.—(The Holocaust)
    Includes bibliographical references and index.
    ISBN 978-0-7565-4390-7 (library binding)
    ISBN 978-0-7565-4442-3 (paperback)
    1. Jewish children in the Holocaust—Juvenile literature. 2. Holocaust, Jewish (1939–1945)—
Personal narratives—Juvenile literature.
I. Title. II. Series.
    D804.48.F58 2011
    940.53'18083—dc22   2010019975

Visit Compass Point Books on the Internet at www.capstonepub.com

Printed in the United States of America in Stevens Point, Wisconsin.
072011
006285R

Table of Contents

Preface

In 1933 an Austrian-born politician named Adolf Hitler became the chancellor of Germany. Hitler was the leader of the National Socialist German Workers Party—the Nazi Party. Hitler was bitterly anti-Semitic and blamed the Jews for Germany's economic problems.

Hitler dreamed of populating Europe with Aryans, members of what he called a master race. The Aryans included Germans with fair skin, blond hair, and blue eyes. Hitler believed Jews were the enemy of the Aryans, and he developed a plan to isolate and kill them. Hitler called his plan the Final Solution of the Jewish Question.

With Hitler in power, life for Jewish people in Germany became increasingly difficult and dangerous. By the mid-1930s, Jewish businesses were boycotted and vandalized. Jewish Germans were forced to identify themselves by wearing the Star of David on their clothing. Jewish children were expelled from German schools. Jews were forced to leave their homes and live in certain areas, apart from Aryans, and they lost their German citizenship. Hitler's police beat and killed some Jews on the streets.

The Nazis sent millions of Jews to concentration camps in many parts of Europe. Some camps were killing centers; others were prison and forced-labor camps. Prisoners were beaten and subjected to painful experiments in which they could be maimed or killed. Survival was rare. Prisoners who were not killed in the gas chambers or shot by guards often died of starvation or illness. Besides Jews, the camps held political prisoners, homosexuals, Jehovah's Witnesses, disabled people, and people who were called gypsies.

Hitler's troops invaded Austria, Czechoslovakia, and Poland, and France and Great Britain declared war on Germany September 3, 1939. World War II became a fight between the Allies—led by France, Great Britain, the United States, and the Soviet Union—and the Axis powers of Germany, Italy, and Japan.

Until their defeat in 1945, the Nazis killed 11 million people in more than a dozen countries. Six million were Jews—two-thirds of the Jewish population in Europe. More than a million Jewish children were killed. This genocide became known as the Holocaust.

CHAPTER 1

> To Hitler, children were enemies.
> Children are the future, and he
> wanted to erase all that.
>
> —*Tova Friedman, who survived the
> Holocaust as a child*

Adolf Hitler

HATRED LEADS TO MURDER

When Thomas Buergenthal was 6 years old, he and his family were forced to live in a Jewish ghetto in Kielce, Poland. Two years later all of the children in the ghetto were taken from their families. Thomas survived because he told Nazi officers that he was able to work. He later wrote about the fate of the other children:

We learned later that ... about 30 other children ... were first

locked up in a nearby house. From there, in the late afternoon,

they were taken to the Jewish cemetery, where they were killed.

We heard afterward that the soldiers used hand grenades to

murder them.

It's difficult to tell the story of Jewish children during the Holocaust because few survived the experience. Widespread persecution of Jews began as soon as Adolf Hitler came to power. As the Nazis worked to make their empire, called the Third Reich, *judenfrei*—free of Jews—Jewish people experienced ever-increasing pressure. Jews were persecuted, beaten, imprisoned, and killed.

Later Jews all across Nazi-controlled Europe were transported to concentration camps, where many of them were worked to death in the service of the Reich. Exceptions were made for the very old, the very young, and anyone else considered unfit for hard labor. Usually they were killed upon arrival at the camps.

At the start of World War II, about 1.6 million Jewish children were living in Europe. Fewer than one in 10 of them survived Hitler's reign of terror. More than 100,000 did survive, however— through a combination of strength, cleverness, the help of others, and—more often than not—simple good luck.

Mounting Pressure

Anti-Semitism—prejudice or discrimination against Jewish people—is one of the defining characteristics of Adolf Hitler and the Nazi Party. When the Nazis came to power, there were Jewish people throughout Europe. For many of them, the growing and violent anti-Semitism came as a shock.

Hilde Scheraga, who was born in Frankfurt am Main, Germany, was 3 years old when Hitler came to power in 1933. "From that moment on our destiny would be controlled by the most evil man who ever lived," she said after the war. "He hated the Jews and was intent on getting rid of them. If he could not get rid of them by forcing them to move from Germany then he would have them shot or murdered in [gas chambers]. We did not yet know this. We did not yet know that our destiny was to be murdered, that our crime was being Jewish, and that our punishment was death."

On April 1, 1933, the Nazis ordered a boycott of Jewish businesses in Germany. It was their first nationwide action against the Jewish Germans. Lists of Jewish-owned businesses were distributed in every town. The word *Jude*—German for "Jew"—was painted on signs that were affixed to storefronts. The Star of David and swastikas were painted on store windows. Crude messages such as "Don't Buy from Jews" and "The Jews Are Our Misfortune" were written on storefronts. Just in case shoppers didn't get the message, members of the Nazi Party's private army—the Sturmabteilung (SA)—were stationed in front of Jewish shops to discourage people from entering. Despite these efforts, however, the boycott was not very successful and was abandoned after just one day. The failure did not end Nazi pressure, though. In fact, things steadily got worse.

Over the following weeks and years, the Nazis imposed laws that, among other things, limited where Jews could work and go to school. In 1934 and 1935, Jewish Germans lost the right to go

SA pickets handed boycott pamphlets to those who passed by a shop owned by Jewish Germans.

to many public places, including hotels, theaters, restaurants, and sports arenas. Jewish doctors were not allowed to treat non-Jewish patients. Jewish attorneys no longer could practice law.

Jewish youngsters also lost the normal joys of childhood. They were no longer allowed to visit movie theaters, parks, or swimming pools. Most of their non-Jewish friends no longer spoke to them. Ursula Rosenfeld, who was 7 years old when Hitler came to power, remembers when she first realized that something was terribly wrong. It was the day her mother had planned to have a birthday party for her.

"The table was set. … I was sort of very excited," Rosenfeld later said. "Nobody came. Not a single child came to this birthday party. And so, that was the first terrible blow to me. I know it sounds trivial, but it was the first sort of comprehension for a child to understand that you're ostracized, that there's something different about you."

Of course there was nothing different about Ursula and other Jewish children, but being ignored was awful. However, it was often better than the alternative. Jack Hellman has vivid memories of how non-Jewish children treated him.

"I feared every day," he said. "I just was most unhappy going to school. [Once when] I was walking on the street, six or seven boys came, called me 'Jew bastard,' and then attacked me and threw me through a plate-glass window. I was cut severely, and I had to go to the hospital for stitching and I didn't want to go to the school there anymore. … I just felt that I was threatened constantly."

On September 15, 1935, anti-Semitic discrimination in Germany was formalized in the Nuremberg Laws. The laws declared that Jewish Germans were not citizens. It also prohibited them from marrying non-Jews or even employing Aryans as household help.

Most German Jewish children went to regular public schools until laws forbade them to do so.

Under the Nuremberg Laws, a Jew was not defined as someone belonging to a particular religious group. The Nazis considered Jews a separate—and inferior—ethnic group. Anyone who had three or four Jewish grandparents was considered a Jew, whether that person practiced the Jewish religion or not. Even people who had converted to Christianity were defined as Jews if they had three or four Jewish grandparents.

The Nazis' goal at the time was to make Germany judenfrei. They were not yet focused on killing every Jewish person they could. By making life difficult for Jewish people, the Nazis hoped they would force them to leave the country. The plan worked, to an extent. About 282,000 Jews left Germany from January 1933 through September 1939. Still, more than 200,000 remained.

But emigration in the late 1930s became more difficult. Some Jews wanted to leave Germany and its neighboring countries, but they were unable to. A Jewish person who wanted to leave Germany had to have a sponsor in the country where he or she was going. Then he or she had to get a visa from that country to be allowed in, as well as an exit permit from the Nazis. All of this paperwork had to be collected and presented within a certain time period. It was nearly impossible. It was also very expensive. Many people couldn't

As part of a peace agreement after World War I, Palestine was given to the United Kingdom to govern. From the 1920s on, many Jewish people had immigrated to Palestine, where they hoped to create a Jewish state. Many Jews wanted to leave Nazi Germany and settle in Palestine, but the United Kingdom had strict immigration policies that prevented the Jews from entering.

afford it. But there was another problem. As Lore Segal, who was a child in Vienna at the time, noted, "The hardest thing was to find a country to go to."

Many countries had strict immigration policies that limited the number of people allowed in. In the 1930s, during the Great Depression, people worried that the few jobs available in their countries would be taken by immigrants. They also worried that immigrants without jobs would need too much help from the government. Many experts believe anti-Semitism also played a role in the tight controls on how many Jewish immigrants could be accepted.

In March 1938 a union called the *Anschluss* was created when Germany annexed Austria. When Austria's population was incorporated into the Reich, the number of Jews in Germany increased by about 185,000. In September Britain, France, and Italy allowed Germany to take over a part of Czechoslovakia called the Sudetenland. This area was home to a large minority of German-speaking people. Once again Germany's Jewish population increased. Two months later the Nazi leadership decided to put more pressure on Jews to make them leave Nazi-controlled territory.

The Night of Broken Glass

During the night of November 9, 1938, members of the Nazi Party and the Nazis' private army, the SA, went on a violent rampage.

The Evian Conference

U.S. President Franklin Roosevelt called for an international conference to discuss what to do about Jewish citizens in Nazi-controlled lands. The conference began in July 1938. Representatives from 31 countries met in Evian-les-Bains, France, to find a solution. Only one of the countries represented at the conference—the Dominican Republic—was willing to lift its immigration restrictions and accept more Jewish refugees.

A worker cleared broken glass from a Jewish store following the anti-Jewish riots of Kristallnacht.

They destroyed just about everything that was owned by Jews. Almost 8,000 Jewish-owned stores, businesses, and homes were destroyed. Hundreds of synagogues were ransacked and burned. Hundreds of Jews were murdered. About 30,000 Jewish men and boys were arrested and eventually sent to concentration camps.

The November pogrom came to be known as Kristallnacht—meaning "the night of broken glass"—because the streets were littered with shattered windows from the Jewish homes, businesses, and synagogues that had been destroyed. "I was 8 years old when these pogroms took place," Hilde Scheraga recalled. "I will never forget the absolute fear and terror I experienced."

The morning after the pogrom, 13-year-old Ursula Rosenfeld went to school. Everyone was standing in the playground watching the synagogue across the street burn. "Suddenly somebody said, 'Oh there's a Jew, let's throw her on the fire as well,'" Rosenfeld remembered. "I don't know how I got home. I still don't know today how I got home."

CHAPTER 2

Kindertransport child

GLIMMER OF HOPE FOR THE CHILDREN

J ust days after Kristallnacht, the British Jewish Refugee Committee met with Prime Minister Neville Chamberlain and urged him to help the Jews in Germany. Less than a week later, a plan was presented to the House of Commons. It was approved that evening. Britain would relax its immigration rules, but only for children younger than 17. A rescue program was devised. The children selected for this rescue program would be allowed to leave Nazi-controlled areas in Europe to be relocated in Britain. The program became known as the Kindertransport. *Kinder* is the German word for children.

The movement of the children began in December 1938. The last group left September 1, 1939—two days before Britain entered World War II. During that time about 10,000 children traveled out of Nazi Germany, Austria, Poland, and Czechoslovakia to Great Britain. Each child came alone, with just one suitcase, a small bag, and a sign with a number hanging from a string around his or her neck.

For the parents, the decision to send a child away without knowing where he or she would end up—or whether they would ever see the child again—was agonizing. By 1938, however, many parents were beginning to realize that it might be their children's only chance for survival. Franzi Groszmann sent her 10-year-old daughter Lore away. She never forgot how difficult that decision was.

"The hurt is unbelievable," she said many years later. "That cannot be described."

For the children, many of whom were too young to understand what was happening, being forced to leave home was crushing. "The parting was terrible," remembers Ursula Rosenfeld. "That's the one thing I've never forgotten in all my life."

Life Among Strangers

The children who had sponsors—people who paid for their passage and would provide a home—were sent to London. Many others were sent to a summer vacation camp called Dovercourt Bay until a place could be found for them. Many families opened their homes to the Jewish children and treated them like their own children. But some children had unpleasant experiences with hosts who were unkind or who made them work as servants. Sometimes the children had a difficult time adjusting to their hosts—and vice versa.

"None of the foster parents with whom I stayed, and there were five of them, none of them could stand me for very long," recalled Lore Segal. "But all of them had the grace to take in a Jewish child. They were not particularly warm. They did not love me. I did not love them. Nevertheless, they did, as I say, what most of us don't do, which is to burden the household, the kitchen, the bedroom, and

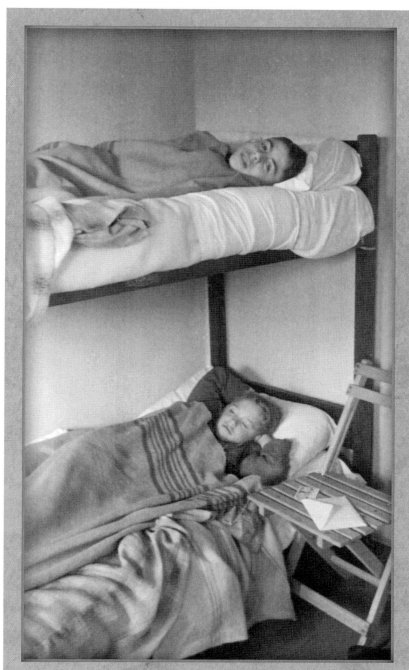

Two boys who were part of the Kindertransport program bunked at
Dovercourt Bay, a vacation camp near Harwich, England.

the living room, with this little foreigner."

"The children whom we brought over and placed I think, in the main, were satisfactory," said Sir Nicholas Winton, one of the British organizers of the transport program. "There were certainly some who were misused and used as servants if they were of the right age. I wouldn't claim that it was a 100 percent success, but I would claim that everybody who came over was alive at the end of the war." The same could not be said for the children who remained in Nazi-controlled Europe. As many as 1.5 million Jewish children were killed in the Holocaust.

Parents sent their children away with promises to join them in England soon. In letters, the parents urged their children to be good and reminded them that they would soon be reunited.

The Wagner-Rogers Child Refugee Bill

The destruction and imprisonments of Kristallnacht left about 20,000 children homeless and fatherless. In January 1939 Senator Robert Wagner of New York and Representative Edith Rogers of Massachusetts introduced a bill in Congress to grant those 20,000 children entry to the United States. A Gallup poll conducted at the time showed that two-thirds of the American public opposed the idea. The bill never made it to the floor of either the House or Senate; it was killed in committee.

For all of the Kinder, that promise was what kept them going. Many tried desperately to get British citizens to sponsor their parents' immigration. Lorraine Allard was 14 when she joined the Kindertransport. From the moment she arrived in England, she went to every large house she could find and begged for jobs for her parents. When someone finally agreed, Lorraine said, "it was like an unbelievable dream come true." As British officials worked on the

Many Jewish children found temporary homes with British families during the Kindertransport program.

A young boy wrote to his parents while he was at Dovercourt Bay.

necessary documents, however, war was declared. Immigration was

stopped. Lorraine was crushed.

"I just felt the world come to an end," she said. "Shattering, if

I think about it, because everything was built around this reunion and my temporary stay in England. Everything we'd ever talked about or written about it, thought about it, had all collapsed. Everything had collapsed. I think I cried for, not weeks, not months, I cried for years."

After the war began, regular mail between Kinder and their parents ended. Correspondence was limited to 25-word Red Cross postcards. For many children, the postcards eventually stopped coming—and they had no idea why.

When the war in Europe ended, Lorraine could hardly contain her excitement. "I just thought, 'Well this is it. I'm going to see my parents next week,'" she recalled. Lorraine immediately sent messages to the last known address of each of her parents. "The letters were returned to me about three, four months later—took a long time," she said. "All it said on the back: 'Deported to Auschwitz, October '44.' The war was finished in May '45. That's how I found out [that my parents were dead]."

Like Lorraine, most of the Kindertransport children never saw their parents again.

CHAPTER 3

Boy eating soup in Lodz, Poland, ghetto

The ghetto was the beginning
of my conscious terror.

—*Tova Friedman, child survivor*

LIFE AND DEATH IN THE GHETTOS

Making Germany free of Jews was only one part of Hitler's plan. He also wanted to create a vast empire. The Anschluss and the takeover of the Sudetenland, in western Czechoslovakia, were just the first steps.

In March 1939 Nazi forces invaded Czechoslovakia. On September 1 they invaded Poland. For the next year, the Nazis continued their march across Europe. But when the Nazis gained new territory, the Jewish population of the

Reich increased. One way for Nazi officers to reduce these numbers was to murder entire villages of people. Judy Altman was 14 years old when Czechoslovakia was invaded. Her sister, Charlotte, lived across the border in Poland. Every week Judy's mother would send a peasant to deliver food to Charlotte's family.

"One day the peasant returned," Judy said, "and he said, 'I regret very much not being able to deliver the food to Charlotte, but I witnessed her execution.' The Germans had gathered all the Jews in

In the fall of 1939, Hitler ordered what was called the "mercy killing" of sick and disabled people in Germany. This program was code-named T4. At first the Nazis eliminated newborns and very young children. Doctors and midwives were required to report any child under the age of 3 who showed signs of physical deformity, mental retardation, or another so-called ailment. Parents whose children had these symptoms were encouraged to bring them to special clinics. In reality the clinics were killing centers. The program was soon expanded to include older children and adults suffering from mental or chronic illness. Victims were killed by starvation, lethal medication, or gassing. T4 served as training for operating the gas chambers that would later be used in death camps across the Reich.

Ghettos for Jews in Nazi-occupied Europe

the town, made them dig a mass grave, made them undress naked,

and shot the children first, then the husbands and the mothers."

Inside the Walls

At a conference in Berlin on September 21, 1939, Nazi officials

devised a new plan for dealing with the Jews in Poland. Many would

be rounded up and forced to live in ghettos.

Ghettos were small districts inside a city where Jewish people

were forced to live under terrible conditions. They were controlled

A group of children in front of a makeshift shelter in a Polish ghetto.

by the Schutzstaffel. Originally formed as a security force for Hitler, the SS had evolved by 1934 into the Nazi Party's most ruthless private police force. The SS's Death's Head Units were put in charge of the concentration camps, and more than 1 million SS men formed a second army during World War II.

The ghettos were designed to round up the Jews in one area and isolate them. A closed ghetto, the most common type, was separated from the rest of the city by walls or fences topped with barbed wire. Open ghettos didn't have walls, but the ability to leave or enter them was restricted.

The living conditions were the same in most of the ghettos—

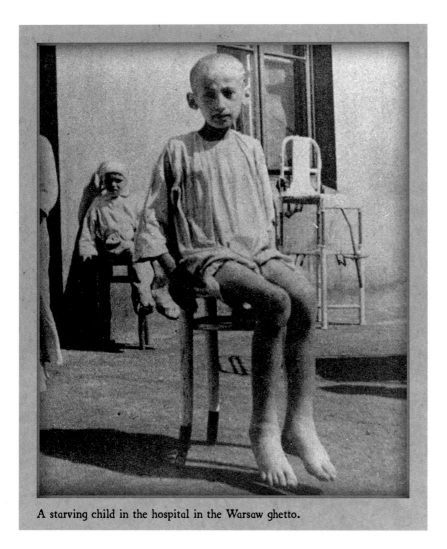

A starving child in the hospital in the Warsaw ghetto.

they were overcrowded, unsanitary, and harshly governed. The

Warsaw ghetto was the largest in Poland. More than 400,000 Jews

were jammed into a 1.3 square-mile (3.4 square-kilometer) area.

That's about the same size as New York City's Central Park. There

was seldom enough food or heat to keep the people healthy, and

disease spread quickly. In the Warsaw ghetto, 83,000 Jews died from hunger or disease. Many others were worked to death or killed by German officials. Most of the remaining Jews were sent to death camps. Tova Friedman was 4 years old when her family was forced to live in a ghetto in Tomaszow-Mazowiecki, Poland. "That marks my first real memories of the terror and the hunger and the disappearance of people," she said. "Nobody knew where they went, but we knew we would never see them again."

One day officials gathered everyone in the ghetto and brought them to an open space. "They just shot most of the people, and other people were put on some kind of trains," Tova recalled. "I remember people screaming and yelling and crying and holding onto each other." Tova's grandparents were among those murdered in the ghetto. Tova and her parents were part of a small group left alive. Asked how she escaped death, Tova says, "There is no answer. We weren't smarter. We weren't better. I don't know. Life was a nightmare with all kinds of rules that you didn't know what they were. There were six buildings in that ghetto, then there were four buildings, then there were two buildings left with people. They could've started with our building; instead they started with the other. It is not possible to ask a logical question about an illogical time."

Those left alive were sent to a new ghetto. It was a labor camp, where everyone had to work for the Germans. Labor camps were particularly dangerous for children. The people living there were supposed to work. As far as the Nazis were concerned, anyone who couldn't work—such as elderly people and children—didn't deserve to live.

Tova survived life in the labor camp because her father created a hiding space for her in the attic of their home. One evening Tova's parents hurried her into the hiding spot. The SS had rounded up the residents of the ghetto and were putting all of the children on a truck.

"Some of the parents went on the truck with the children," Tova remembered. "Some of the younger kids … the parents would not allow their kids to go, and they held onto them. So the Germans just kept pulling until they dismembered the children. I was sitting on my mother's lap, and she put her hand on my mouth because she thought I would scream and give away our hiding place. After hours and hours of watching this, I said to myself, 'OK, I'm the last Jewish child left on earth.'"

On most days people were taken from the ghettos. Some were sent to extermination camps. Others were simply killed. Beginning in late 1941, the Nazis were ready to begin their "final solution." Entire ghettos were emptied of people. From then on, many Jews were taken from all across Europe to extermination camps in Poland, including Auschwitz-Birkenau, Belzec, Chelmno, Sobibor, and Treblinka.

CHAPTER 4

Siblings in hiding in Italy

> If [the Germans] had caught us, first they
> would have shot my children right before
> my eyes, then the child we were hiding,
> and then they would have killed us.
>
> —Genowefa Nowak, non-Jewish Polish rescuer

LIFE IN HIDING

As time passed it became increasingly obvious to everyone that the Nazis had no use for most Jewish children. Rescue networks and resistance groups worked feverishly to save as many youngsters as they could. Desperate parents mostly appealed to people they knew and trusted to save their children. Children who could pass as non-Jewish sometimes became parts of new families. These were usually children who had light hair, light skin, and light

The false birth certificate of Teresa Wieczorkowska, which was used by Dawid Tennenbaum, a Jewish boy living in hiding as a girl in Lvov, Poland

eyes. Others had to stay hidden at all times.

No one knows how many children were saved in these ways. What is known is that many people across Nazi-controlled Europe risked their lives to save the lives of the children. The punishment for harboring Jews was well known. At best, those found guilty would be sent to concentration camps. At worst, they would be killed immediately.

In many cases, the people who risked their lives to save children cared deeply for them, even though they were often strangers at first. Though many of the children also grew to care for their rescuers, it was a difficult and confusing time for them. Many felt abandoned by their parents, confused by their new identities, and afraid of being discovered.

One of the Family

Adam and Julia Melcer lived in the Warsaw ghetto with their daughter Alice. Day after day, they watched the population shrink as more people were sent to the Treblinka death camp. They realized they had to do something to save their 3-year-old child.

"I knew she was going to die," Julia recalled. "They were going to kill her. I was so worried, my heart was burning. People did not want to believe it. They think, 'No, the Germans wouldn't do that.' Only, I believed it."

One day a man came to the Melcers and offered to take Alice to safety. "We had no other choice," Adam said later. "This was the only way to save her life."

Rudolf and Jochébed Hilfman, on the other hand, didn't believe the horror stories that were circulating. Johanna and Aart Vos, non-Jews who, like the Hilfmans, lived in Amsterdam, offered four times to hide the family, but Rudolf Hilfman repeatedly said no. Finally the Voses persuaded him to give them his 4-year-old daughter, Moana. Her suitcase was packed, and she was told she was going on vacation. The young child had no idea she was saying good-bye to her parents forever.

Although Moana grew to love Johanna and Aart Vos—and they her—it was a confusing time for the child. "I cannot say to you that this was a really happy time to me," she later explained. "It was not, because I didn't understand at all why

Guta Tyrangiel posed with Bronislawa and Josef Jaszczuk, the Polish couple who hid her during the war.

my parents weren't coming to get me. I felt very much abandoned by them. I thought that I was [being] punished by them."

The Voses had two daughters of their own when they took in Moana. Barbara, who was 4 years old, loved having a new playmate. Six-year-old Hetty felt differently about the situation—though she, too, considered Moana her sister. "I have been angry most of my life," Hetty says. "The thing that I've resented for so long, the thing that I've been so angry about, is the fact that [our parents] risked our lives, as well as their own." It was not just adults who could be punished for hiding a Jewish child—the entire family could suffer the same fate.

In the Dark

Ephraim "Fred" Gat was 5 years old when he went into hiding in Poland with the Nowak family. "We didn't think about the danger, we just wanted to save the child," explained Genowefa Nowak. "A simple thing."

The Nowaks occupied two rooms in a crowded apartment building. If they were found to be hiding a Jew, everyone in the building could be punished.

Since he couldn't pass as a non-Jew, Fred spent most of his time sitting in a tiny closet. He couldn't get up, he couldn't sneeze, he

A Dutch policeman crouched inside a bunker that served as a hiding place for Dutch Jews in 1942 and 1943.

couldn't even go to the bathroom until it was safe to come out. "Most of the time I felt [like] a zombie," he recalled. Even though he was just a little boy, Fred never complained—and he never made a sound.

The Pain of Surviving

After the war Alice Melcer was reunited with her parents, who had survived imprisonment at Auschwitz and Dachau. Then 5 years old, she had a hard time understanding what was happening. When Alice saw her mother again, Julia had no hair, was terribly thin, and was dressed in rags. Alice wanted nothing to do with her. "I couldn't stand her touching me," she said. "What she looked like when she came back! I didn't believe that she was my mother."

Moana Hilfman was 6 years old at the end of World War II. Her parents, like so many others, had been murdered in the Nazi camps. The Vos family tried to adopt the little girl, but they were not allowed to do so because they weren't Jewish. The Jewish community felt very strongly that Jewish orphans should be placed with Jewish families. Ideally they would be placed with relatives.

In a case in which no family members survived, a child would be adopted by another Jewish family. Moana was sent to live with an aunt and uncle who had survived the war. "Moana was a sister," Hetty said later. "When she was torn away, it was just that. She was torn. She left a hole in our lives."

Aviva Sleslin was 9 months old when a rescuer smuggled her out of a Lithuanian ghetto in a suitcase. She later summed up an experience shared by many hidden children: "Our childhoods had been marked by secrecy, fear, and overwhelming loss. Still, I believe we were lucky. Not only had our rescuers saved our lives, but through their courage and generosity they had shown us, in the midst of evil, humanity at its very best."

CHAPTER 5

Boy in Buchenwald camp clothing

I feared nothing, knew nothing, cared about nothing. I forgot I had a mother. I completely forgot I had anybody.

—*Tova Friedman, child survivor*

SURVIVING THE DEATH CAMPS

Concentration camps were originally built to imprison the Nazis' political

rivals. By 1935 these detention camps also were being used to hold people

the Nazis felt were inferior, such as Jews and those they called gypsies. In

1942 some camps became extermination camps designed to be death factories. When

Germany started losing the war, in 1943, many slave labor camps were created to get

useful work out of the inmates. Many of the inmates were worked to death.

People were often transported from ghettos to the camps in railroad cars with no windows and a door that was bolted shut. So many people were packed into each car that there was no room to sit down. The prisoners often had no food or water. For most, the journey lasted for several days. The stench, the hunger and thirst, and the fear were overwhelming. After four and a half days, Judy Altman and her family arrived at Auschwitz. As the doors opened, the teenager saw prisoners in striped uniforms. "Where are we? What is this?" she asked. "This is hell," someone replied.

Selektion

The first thing that happened to most new prisoners at any camp was *Selektion* (Selection). After the prisoners moved off the trains, SS doctors judged whether they would live or die. Those who were fit for work were ordered to move to one side. Those deemed unfit to work were herded to the other side, then sent directly to the gas chambers to be killed.

Like so many others, Judy Altman and her family faced Dr. Josef Mengele for Selektion. Judy, then 17 years old, lined up with her mother, her sister, her niece, her aunt, and her three young cousins. In the other line were the men: her father, her nephew, her uncle, and her brother-in-law. Judy and her teenage niece were sent to the

A Jewish woman walked toward the gas chambers with three young children after going through Selektion at Auschwitz-Birkenau.

left. The rest of her family was moved to the right.

"As I looked back I saw my mother fainting, falling down, so I went behind the rows to help my mother up," Judy said. "Mengele saw that—somebody dared disobey his order! He grabbed me and threw me to the left. With that gesture, he threw me to life. As I passed my father's row, he put his hand on my head as he did every Friday night to bless the children. And he said to me 'Judy, you will live.' That slogan kept me going, because every time that I felt I

Josef Mengele (right) was a Nazi doctor and SS officer who conducted many medical experiments on concentration camp prisoners. He

was particularly interested in twins. His experiments included injecting chemicals into the children's eyes to see whether they would change color. He also stitched twins together, performed sibling-to-sibling transfusions, and removed people's limbs and organs without using anesthesia. After the experiments Mengele would often kill his subjects to study their organs. He was called the Angel of Death.

At the end of World War II, Mengele escaped justice. For 34 years he used various names and lived in South America. He died in 1979.

could not take it anymore, that I wish I died, I said, 'Oh, no. Daddy said I will live.'"

Tova Friedman and her parents were also sent to Auschwitz. "The biggest miracle of all is why I wasn't killed right when I got off the train at Auschwitz, because there [was a] crematorium right next to us exactly for that purpose—for every child under 12," Tova said. "They never got inside. [The Nazis] didn't want to bother wasting the space. I was certainly in the open—they shaved my head. They treated me like an adult. I was five and a half."

Worked to Death

After Selektion at Auschwitz-Birkenau, the heads of the prisoners chosen for slavery were shaved, and they received thin cotton uniforms and wooden clogs. There was no underwear. Then they were registered. At Birkenau a tattooed number was put on their arms. From then on the number was the prisoner's only identification. Many prisoners were sent to labor camps in other parts of Nazi-occupied Europe.

All around them, the newly arrived prisoners saw inmates who looked like skeletons—people who were being starved and worked to death by their Nazi tormentors. The prisoners lived in barracks, which were brick buildings filled with two- and three-tier wooden bunk beds. Within minutes of arriving at her barracks, Judy Altman was overwhelmed, she says, "by the most horrible stench that you can imagine of burning hair and burning nails." She asked another girl who had been in the camp for a while what was causing the smell. "That is your parents burning," the girl said.

Each morning the prisoners were awakened while it was still dark. They were forced to gather for a head count.

Women in the barracks at Auschwitz

"The worst part of the day was roll call," remembered Jack Mandelbaum, who was 15 years old at the time. "Not only did it mean standing at attention for hours on end, but it was also when prisoners were punished for some slight infraction, or simply terrorized at random. Everyone was forced to watch when a prisoner was beaten, whipped, shot, hanged, or torn apart by the dogs."

In a typical camp, after roll call the prisoners would be given a cup of weak tea and a chunk of bread. Then they would be marched off to perform backbreaking work for 14 hours or more. In the evening, there was another count, then a meal of soup that was almost entirely water. As the war dragged on, meals got even smaller and less frequent.

"The hunger was incredible," remembers Judy Altman. "No human being should experience hunger like that because you become an animal. You become like a vicious animal, willing to do anything for a morsel of food." Toward the end of her stay in the camps, Judy volunteered to move corpses from a huge pile of bodies

Prisoners from the German concentration camp at Mauthausen worked in a quarry to break huge boulders into small stones.

to a mass grave, because each of those workers later got a bowl of soup. Judy gave her soup to her dying niece.

The daily routine was part of the Nazis' extermination-through-work plan. While their prisoners lived, the Germans had the benefit of their labor. Much of the work done by the prisoners supported the operation of the camp. Concentration camp labor

Concentration camp prisoners were forced to build airplane parts for the Germans at a factory in Bobrek, Poland.

also built factories, air raid shelters, roads, airplanes, and rockets. Some workers made tires, uniforms, and other things for the German army. Prisoners also did especially dangerous work, such as making explosives and munitions and clearing unexploded bombs from cities. When workers died, their bodies were sent to the crematoriums. New prisoners arrived at the camps nearly every day. They took the places of those who had died.

Like some of the other young prisoners in the camps, Jack Mandelbaum was determined to survive. "I believed my family was waiting for me," he explained. "When this was over, they would be there, outside the camp, to greet me. And I would have beaten Hitler at his game."

The Death Marches

In 1944 the Allies were winning the war in Europe. That winter, as Soviet, British, and U.S. forces began fighting their way toward the sites of mass murder, German officials tried to erase all evidence of their existence. The SS dismantled many of the crematoriums, gas chambers, and other buildings and tried to evacuate the prisoners. The plan was to take them away from the front and move them to labor camps inside Germany. The prisoners were forced to march many miles in the bitter cold, many of them with only rags wrapped

Two ovens inside the crematorium where bodies were burned in Dachau

around their feet and thin blankets draped over their shoulders.

Anyone who could not keep up was shot. Some people simply fell

down dead on the road from hunger, exposure, or exhaustion.

You are free, but where do you go? You have no parents, no siblings, nothing.

—*Judy Altman, child survivor*

LIBERATION AT LAST

As the Germans rushed to empty the camps, rumors reached the prisoners that Allied forces were on the way. Some prisoners chose to hide to escape the death marches. Tova Friedman's mother was one of them. She knew she would not survive the march, and she did not want to leave her little girl alone in the world. She decided they would hide in the hospital rather than leave the camp.

Tova lay down next to a woman's corpse, and her mother covered her and the dead body with a sheet. Her mother hid under a blanket in another part of the hospital. Tova, wanting to have her doll, clung to the body of the dead woman instead. "That was a piece of cake," she recalled. "When death is an everyday occurrence—and starvation and shooting and all this—when you grow up in this, your mind becomes like old leather. There is a trained behavior that you must follow because the consequences are

Prisoners from Dachau were sent on death marches as the Allied forces moved closer to liberating the camp.

irrevocable. You'll just be dead, and that's the end of that."

Tova listened, silent, as other prisoners were dragged out of the hospital. Those who could not walk were shot. Finally she fell asleep. Then Tova's mother took her out of the hospital. In the distance, they saw SS troops marching the prisoners away from the camp. Before long the Soviet Army arrived. They were free.

Like many liberated prisoners, Tova and her mother did not know what to do with their freedom. They had been moved far from their homes to the concentration camps. Some former prisoners didn't even know where they were. Tova and her mother stayed in the camp for a few months and then were able to board a Red Cross truck that was heading north. They hoped to eventually make their way home to Tomaszow, Poland.

The Little Camp

Beginning in the middle of 1944, children were evacuated from camps in the east and taken to Buchenwald, a camp near Weimar, Germany. The youngest child was just 2 years old. In January 1945 prisoners forced to help run the camp secretly set aside Block 66 to rescue young boys and teens. The youngsters were not assigned to labor, and they received slightly more nourishing food than what was given to the rest of the prisoners.

American troops liberated Buchenwald April 11, 1945. The
soldiers searched the barracks. When they reached Block 66, they
were shocked by what they saw: hundreds of skeletal children.

Young survivors in the Buchenwald concentration camp

The commander of the American troops sent a message to the children's rescue group Oeuvre de Secours aux Enfants in Geneva, Switzerland, asking for help in evacuating the children.

The organization arranged for 280 children to go to Switzerland, 250 to England, and 480 to France. The children left Buchenwald in June. In the meantime, American troops gave the boys food and clothing. The soldiers were so upset by the children's condition that they tried to give them as much food as possible. But the children's bodies couldn't handle the rich food. Some got sick, and some died. The same thing happened to prisoners of all ages at the other liberated camps.

Like other survivors, the boys had trouble adjusting to normal life. To them adults represented the enemy, because adults were to blame for what had happened. They talked very little to outsiders. Most of the boys were just waiting to start their new lives in Palestine. They wanted to get as far away from Germany as possible. Their most pressing concern, however, was finding their families. For most of them, the search would be in vain.

Going Home

After his camp was liberated, 11-year-old Thomas Buergenthal traveled with the Polish army until he reached a Jewish orphanage

Elie Wiesel (right) was one of the boys rescued from Buchenwald's Block 66 and sent to live in France. He later discovered that his parents, little sister, and grandmother had all been killed on arrival at Auschwitz. After the war he wrote *Night*, a book about his

experiences in Auschwitz and Buchenwald. As his fame grew, Wiesel used his influence to fight for oppressed people around the world. In 1984 Wiesel was awarded the U.S. Congressional Gold Medal in recognition of his commitment to human rights. Two years later he was awarded the Nobel Peace Prize. In his acceptance speech, he said: "Wherever men or women are persecuted because of their race, religion, or political views, that place must—at that moment—become the center of the universe."

in Poland. "Even though I had seen many people die in the camps, it never occurred to me that my parents might not be alive," he wrote. "I was sure that they would find me as soon as they were liberated."

Like Thomas, many of those who survived held onto the dream that one day they would return home and be reunited with their loved ones. Instead most were faced with a grim reality. Entire families had been wiped out by the Nazis. Those who returned to their homes found they were either destroyed or occupied by strangers who resented being asked to give up what they considered their property. Many freed prisoners once again experienced the anti-Semitism that had started their ordeal. When Tova Friedman returned to Poland in 1946, she said later, "The Poles were vicious. They called us 'dirty Jews' and threw stones at us." The little girl, then 6, tried to go to school, but she couldn't focus on her studies.

After the war there were violent anti-Jewish riots called pogroms in some Polish cities. The worst pogrom took place in Kielce in July 1946. After about 150 Jews returned to the village, the people who had been living there worried that more Jews would come to reclaim their possessions. The survivors were attacked by mobs. More than 40 people were killed, and about 50 were wounded. As news of the pogrom spread, survivors realized that they no longer had a home in Poland.

Some survivors lived in displaced-persons camps while they looked for permanent homes. Many survivors hoped to immigrate to Palestine, which they considered their homeland. Others hoped to gain entry to the United States or other countries. At first many countries refused to change their immigration policies to admit more refugees. Great Britain, which controlled Palestine, still

With nowhere else to go, many Jewish children ended up in displaced-persons camps at the end of the war.

refused to admit large numbers of Jews. Then the United Nations

voted to divide Palestine into a Jewish state and an Arab state. The

British began withdrawing from the region in early 1948. On

May 14 the formation of the state of Israel was announced. After

that Jewish refugees were free to settle in Palestine. The United

States relaxed its immigration policies to allow more Jewish refugees

to settle there as well.

Many survivors tried to bury the past. Some found, and still

find, their experiences impossible to talk about. Others believe that speaking about the Holocaust is a way to honor those who perished. "By keeping this alive," Tova Friedman explains, "these people have not just disappeared for nothing."

Some survivors have dedicated their lives to helping other oppressed people and to making sure a horrendous event like the Holocaust is never repeated. "I can't pay back or thank some of the people who helped me," explained Hedy Epstein, one of the Kindertransport children, "but I can do something for other people."

Judy Altman speaks to schoolchildren about her experiences. She does it, she said, to spread an important message. "When I come to the schools, I tell the children two things: If you see anybody hurting one another, stand up," she said. "Don't just stand there and say, 'It doesn't concern me,' because it does. More important: Do not carry hate, because hate destroys you, not the hated one. He doesn't know it, and you don't achieve anything. Use your energy to be a good human being and help humanity in every way you can."

March 1933

Dachau concentration camp opens to imprison political opponents

April 1933

Most Jewish students are banned from universities and public high schools in Germany

September 15, 1935

The Nuremberg Laws are enacted, depriving Jews of their citizenship and other basic rights

November 15, 1938

All Jewish children are expelled from public schools in Germany and Austria

Great Britain's Kindertransport program begins

December 1938

July 1942

Treblinka II killing center is built in Poland

July 23, 1944

Soviet troops liberate the Majdanek, Poland, death camp

January 27, 1945

Soviet troops liberate Auschwitz

Timeline

Buchenwald
concentration
camp opens

July 16, 1937

November 9-10, 1938

On Kristallnacht, the night
of broken glass, Nazis
terrorize Jews in Germany
and Austria

Auschwitz
concentration
and death camp is
established in Poland

September 1-3, 1939

January 20, 1942

Germany invades Poland,
and World War II begins

May 1940

Nazi leaders meet at
Wannsee, Germany, to
discuss the Final Solution
of the Jewish Question

U.S. troops liberate
Buchenwald; British
troops liberate
Bergen-Belsen

May 8, 1945

April 1945

Germany surrenders,
ending the war in Europe

Glossary

anesthesia—drug that blocks pain or causes a loss of sensation

anti-Semitism—prejudice or discrimination against Jewish people

atrocity—horrible act

boycott—organized refusal to do business with a person or group as a form of protest

crematorium—furnace in which dead bodies are burned, or the building containing it

discrimination—unjust treatment based on a person's race, religion, gender, sexual preference, or age

emigrate—to leave a country to settle in another country permanently

evacuate—to move away from an area or to empty a place or thing

extermination—getting rid of something or someone by killing

genocide—systematic extermination of all or a large portion of a national, racial, religious, or ethnic group

immigrated—settled in a new country

integrated—combined

liberated—set free

ostracized—excluded from a group

persecution—unfair or cruel treatment of a person or group of people

pogrom—organized attack against a minority group, particularly Jewish people

refugees—people who are forced to leave their homes because of persecution, war, or natural disaster

sponsor—someone who pays for another's passage to a new country and promises that the person won't become a burden on the government

Third Reich—official name of the Nazi regime that ruled Germany from 1933 to 1945

visa—document that permits a citizen of one country to travel to and from another country

Additional Resources

Further Reading

Bartoletti, Susan Campbell. *Hitler Youth: Growing Up in Hitler's Shadow*. New York: Scholastic Nonfiction, 2005.

Boas, Jacob. *We Are Witnesses: Five Diaries of Teenagers Who Died in the Holocaust*. New York: Square Fish, 2009.

Haugen, Brenda. *The Holocaust Museum*. Minneapolis: Compass Point Books, 2008.

Kaufman, Lola. *The Hidden Girl*. New York: Scholastic, 2010.

Rubin, Susan Goldman. *The Cat With The Yellow Star: Coming of Age in Terezin*. New York: Holiday House, 2006.

Schloss, Eva. *The Promise: The Moving Story of a Family in the Holocaust*. New York: Penguin Global, 2008.

Internet Sites

Use FactHound to find Internet sites related to this book.
All of the sites on FactHound have been researched by our staff.

Here's all you do:
Visit *www.facthound.com*
Type in this code: 9780756543907

Select Bibliography

Altman, Judy. Personal interview. 9 Feb. 2010.

Buergenthal, Thomas. *A Lucky Child: A Memoir of Surviving Auschwitz as a Young Boy*. New York: Little, Brown & Company, 2007.

"Children and the Holocaust." 26 July 2010. http://frank.mtsu. edu/~baustin/children.html

Friedman, Tova. Telephone interview. 10 March 2010.

Gilbert, Martin. *The Boys: The Untold Story of 732 Young Concentration Camp Survivors*. New York: Henry Holt, 1997.

Hemmendinger, Judith. *Survivors: Children of the Holocaust*. Bethesda, Md.: National Press, 1986.

Holocaust Education & Archive Research Team. "The Jews of Sudetenland." 26 July 2010. www.holocaustresearchproject.org/ nazioccupation/sudetenland.html

Holocaust Encyclopedia. United States Holocaust Memorial Museum. www.ushmm.org/wlc/en/

Into the Arms of Strangers: Stories of the Kindertransport. DVD. Warner Brothers Pictures, 2000.

The Kindertransport Association. 26 July 2010. www.kindertransport.org/

Nieuwsma, Milton J., ed. *Kinderlager: An Oral History of Young Holocaust Survivors*. New York: Holiday House, 1998.

Palestine Facts. "What Was the Evian Conference?" 26 July 2010. www.palestinefacts.org/pf_mandate_evian.php

Scheraga, Hilde M., ed. *Childhood Memories: Jewish Children Who Survived the Nazi Peril Speak*. Stamford, Conn.: Holocaust Child Survivors of Connecticut, 1998.

Secret Lives: Hidden Children and Their Rescuers in World War II. DVD. Wellspring, 2003.

The Southern Institute for Education and Research. "Kristallnacht." 26 July 2010. www.southerninstitute.info/holocaust_education/ ds5.html

United States Holocaust Memorial Museum. "The Evian Conference." 26 July 2010. www.ushmm.org/outreach/en/article. php?ModuleId=10007698

Warren, Andrea. *Surviving Hitler: A Boy in the Nazi Death Camps*. New York: Harper Collins, 2001.

Source Notes

Chapter 1: Tova Friedman. Telephone interview. 10 March 2010.

Chapter 2: *Into the Arms of Strangers: Stories of the Kindertransport.* DVD. Warner Brothers Pictures, 2000.

Chapter 3: Tova Friedman.

Chapter 4: Anti-Defamation League, Survivors of the Shoah Visual History Foundation, Yad Vashem. "Rescuers and Non-Jewish Resistance: Those Who Dared to Rescue." 24 Aug. 2010. www.adl.org/tribute_to_rescuers/Those_Who_Dared_Rescue.pdf

Chapter 5: Tova Friedman.

Chapter 6: Judy Altman. Personal interview. 9 Feb. 2010.

About the Author

Stephanie Fitzgerald has been writing nonfiction for children for more than 10 years. Her specialties include history, wildlife, and popular culture. Stephanie is currently working on a picture book with the help of her daughter, Molly.

Index